30 Studies for Flute Solo

Op. 107

by

Sigfrid Karg-Elert

EDITION
FLEURY

EDITION
FLEURY

30 Studies, Op. 107
Flute

1

Allegro alla Händel (non troppo brillante). (Im Händelschen Allegrozeitmaß (nicht zu brillant)).

f grave il suono
(mit breitem Ton)

grazioso
(zierlich)

f senza risoluzione
(ohne Nachschlag)

Appassionato e stretto (♩).(Leidenschaftlich, treibend (rasche ganze Takte.)

brillante
(brillant)

Da capo al 𝄌.

4

Rapido e brillante. (Rasch und glänzend.)

9.

Leggero, grazioso e veloce. (Locker, zierlich, geschwind.)

8

Mosso e leggerissimo. (Sehr leichthin, schwebend.)

5.

10

Un poco mosso, umoristico. (Etwas lebhaft, mit Humor.)

16.

Leggero veloce, giocoso. (Leicht, spielend, sehr rasch.)

17.

11

Adagio (quasi cadenza). (Adagio (im Stile einer Kadenz).)

18.

con fuoco (sehr heftig) — fallargando (breit) vivace (lebhaft)

14

Un pochettino mosso (ben articolato). (Leise bewegt (deutlich phrasiert).)

27.

18

Chaconne.
(Basso ostinato.)

30.

Var. I.

Var. II.

Var. III.

Var. IV.

Var. V.

Var. VI.

20

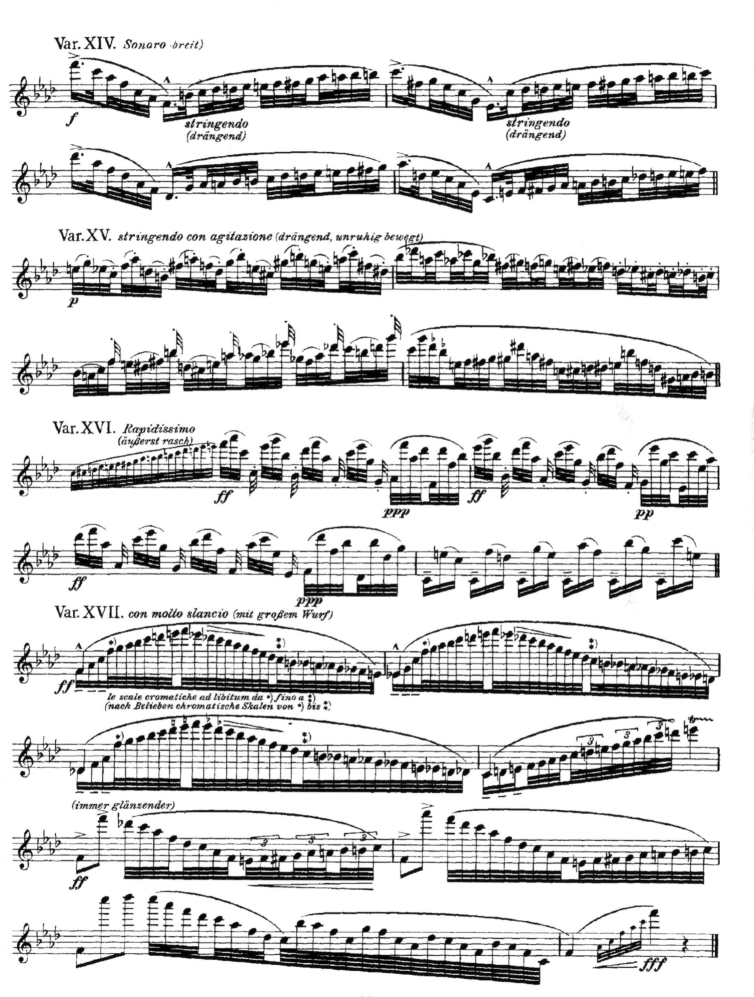

22

NOTES

NOTES

NOTES

NOTES

Made in the USA
Las Vegas, NV
27 April 2023

71171757R00017